THE INCOMPARABLE FESTIVAL

The Incomparable Festival

Mir Yar Ali 'Jan Sahib'

Edited by Razak Khan
Translated by Shad Naved

PENGUIN BOOKS
An imprint of Penguin Random House

PENGUIN BOOKS

USA | Canada | UK | Ireland | Australia
New Zealand | India | South Africa | China

Penguin Books is part of the Penguin Random House group of companies
whose addresses can be found at global.penguinrandomhouse.com

Published by Penguin Random House India Pvt. Ltd
4th Floor, Capital Tower 1, MG Road,
Gurugram 122 002, Haryana, India

Penguin
Random House
India

First published in Penguin Books by Penguin Random House India 2021

Introduction copyright © Razak Khan 2021
Translation copyright © Shad Naved 2021

ISBN 9780670093823

Typeset in Adobe Garamond Pro by Manipal Technologies Limited, Manipal
Printed at Replika Press Pvt. Ltd, India

www.penguin.co.in

بهبار علی عرف   جان صاحب ریختی گو

Mir Yar Ali 'Jan Sahib' *Rekhtigo*. Urdu Illustrated Manuscript 1229.

Contents

Introduction

Space, Speech and Subjectivity in
Jan Sahib's *Jashn-e-Benazir*

'Like the physical monuments destroyed in the aftermath of 1857, many poetic monuments were also shattered or buried, but some survive and others may yet be excavated.'[1]

These are the closing words of Ruth Vanita's pioneering book on Rekhti, a genre of poetry in Urdu from late medieval northern India. This book will excavate a trajectory of this poetic monument in colonial times to write the history and politics of space, speech and subjectivity in Urdu literary history based on the locality of the late nineteenth-century princely state of Rampur in northern India. From the dictionary definition by John T. Platts, 'rekhtī (fr. rekhta), s.f. Hindūstānī verse written in the language of women, and expressing the sentiments, &c. peculiar to them. (The two principal writers in this idiom are the poets Rangīn and Jān Sāḥib.)'[2]

This book focuses on the latter poet Mir Yar Ali 'Jan Sahib's' lesser-known but vivid poetic account, written in Urdu in the form of Rekhti, of the festival–fair held at Rampur, entitled *Musaddas tahniyat-e-jashn-e-benazir* (Felicitations for the Incomparable Festival, in six-hemistich stanzas) probably written in 1867–68. An important aspect of Jan Sahib's oeuvre is his use of women's domestic speech, describing their habitus and sentiments, as well as his interest in adjacent social worlds.[3] In his Rekhti verse, he blurs the genre boundaries between poetry and fiction, history and life-history, by versifying details about elite personages, distinguished artists and commoners and subalterns, grouped together in the carnivalesque space of the royal festival. His poem, therefore, acquires partly the features of the life-writing genre or *tazkira*, in which he describes the qualities of male, female and transvestite performers, entertainers, singers, musicians, dancers and the pleasures they afford to the participants in the festive space. Thus, the text transplants culture beyond the princely court in the bazaar that sprang around the royal celebration (*jashn*). This latter space was increasingly criticized by the emergent middle-class-reformist print culture in the late nineteenth-century colonial India. This introduction to the text will, therefore, focus on the relationship between space, speech and subjectivity by considering Rekhti poetry within the economy and politics of poetic styles and emotions. Urdu is a particularly productive site to map these issues as it is crisscrossed by the linguistic registers of elite literariness, reformist polemics and the common speech of the lower classes. The contiguity of styles, bodily and verbal, and linguistic registers, high and low, give Urdu a sensibility much vaster than its literary historical description as the language of the 'military camp'. Rekhti is a particularly relevant genre to map the hybridity of space, speech and subjectivity and through which we can pose a new set of questions about gender, caste and class in the making of the Muslim identity in South Asia.[4] Its generic properties also help us to understand its global circulation and the local articulation of what Shahab Ahmed has called the 'Balkan-to-Bengal complex' in his thorough revision of the paradigm of Islamic studies. This introduction will address the questions of space, speech and subjectivity, not through the religious domain of pilgrimage and locality, but instead through the secular domain of the market to bring to light another kind of local *imaginaire* and the histories of patronage and integration functioning within it. The text of the Rekhti poem will be the ground on which this mapping and investigation shall be conducted.

The Economy and Politics of Literary Affect

A quintessential text that invokes the locale of princely Rampur, thereby, evoking its literary centrality (*markaz*), the poem is about the royal festival '*jashn-e-benazir*', first held in 1866 by the Nawab Kalb-e-Ali Khan (1832–87) with the aim of promoting art, culture and trade in the state.[5] This annual festival lasted eight days and was a major venue for local trade and cultural promotion, attracting several guilds of craftsmen and artists, and including a range of performers, men, women and gender-crossers.

Mir Yar Ali 'Jan Sahib' (1818–86) moved to the Rampur state, attracted by its royal patronage, fleeing the post-1857 destruction of Lucknow, and wrote the *Musaddas tahniyat-e-jashn-e-benazir*. Jan Sahib used the Rekhti form in the *musaddas* (six-hemistich stanzas) format to describe the festival and its sights and wonders. In a poetic register, he describes the elite, the distinguished artists and commoners brought together in the festival space, blurring the genre distinction between poetry, history and biography, between poetic conventions and social conventions. Positioned as an ode (*qasida*) in honour of Nawab Kalb-e-Ali Khan, the poem also gives a particularistic word-picture (*muraqqa*) of the various sections of society and recounts (*zikr*) the doings of both the elite and common participants.

This long poem uses Rekhti for a clearly public form of address and memorialization. Its world is frequented by several figures of the marketplace selling their skills, art, artefacts and produce. The participants in the festival range broadly across three categories: the aristocratic elite, the middle-class service gentry and artisans and performers. These are not exclusive categories and we see overlaps between them in the transactional space of the festival-cum-marketplace. The elite are drawn to the lowest classes and the class relationships are renegotiated in this space, if not also transformation in some cases, of social identities. In the poem's narrative, Jan Sahib sits surrounded by all these participants as he recounts his observations which are matched by a commentary in visuals (miniature paintings blending Mughal conventions with company style) included in the manuscript, giving us a lyrical *and* visual archive of affect in a distinctively vernacular space.

In his introduction to a modern edition of the text, Imtiaz Ali Khan Khandara notes that the poet is attentive particularly to caste and kin (*zat-biradari*) associations and qualitative descriptions (*zat va sifat*) without any negative judgement (*manfi-andaz*) in his poetic description.[6] The poem, thus, abuts the tazkira genre which describes the qualities of entertainers, singers, musicians, dancers and craftsmen from specific locales. It expounds on the pleasures afforded by entertainers to audiences, making the gathering a splendid and unparalleled event of princely public culture. In this way, the text presents both the political and socio-cultural aspects of princely Rampur.

The bazaar, as Aditya Behl points out, was both an 'ideational and historical world' and, therefore, remained a 'contested space', for it brought all kinds of socially demarcated and segregated actors in a mutual transactional relationship within its space.[7] The space of the bazaar was characterized particularly by those figures that otherwise remained on the margins of society and yet formed its bedrock by selling their labour. Therefore, the bazaar, as Sudipta Sen puts it, was the 'knot in the fabric of social mediation' that determined as well as potentially undermined social hierarchies. Sen has also written about the Mughal elite's contemptuous attitude towards the market folk (*bazariyan*). They were condemned as 'mean and vile' and, therefore, had to be shunned from elite circles for fear of social contagion and moral corruption.[8] Christopher Bayly's milestone work, *Rulers, Townsmen and Bazaars*, establishes the economic, political and socio-cultural role of the bazaar in Indian history even after the period of colonial ascendency.[9] In his work on fairs and marketplaces, Anand Yang makes the important point that melas or fairs have been studied from the perspective of pilgrimage history in South Asia, but, in fact, fairs were sites of entertainment, pleasure-seeking and popular culture that enriched and interrupted the patterns of everyday life. His work is focused on Bihar where he found many nineteenth-century accounts and reformist polemics against melas, such as those by Syed Zahiruddin who called the Maner mela a 'bacchanalian festival resorted to by lower orders'.[10] It is in the condemned festival space around the market space, peopled with the bazariyan, that Jan Sahib situates his word-picture of an entire social world.

Patron and Performers: Ethnography through Poetic Speech

The poem adopts, what I call, a 'poetic ethnography' mode which deploys and plays with different literary genres with the result that social distinctions between different kinds of entertainments, behavioural qualities and caste groups become caught in the play too.[11] The poetic narrator starts by describing the princely patron:

navvab-e-namdar ke jalva julus ka
har husn se zyada hai shaukat ka martaba
Jamshed hi nigodey ka kya jashn-e-mal tha
qurban aydi choti pe us ko karun buwa

asbab jashn ka hai jo logo janab men
Jamshed ne to dekha na hoga yeh khvab men

paushak-e-fakhira voh rafiqon ke bar men hai
jama hai jo harir se behtar nazar men hai
ek ik ghadi bhi sone ki ik ik kamar men hai
zarrin kamar ghulam har ik gharq zar men hai
sarkar ki 'ayan hai yeh dariyadili ka faiz
Hatim to kya na hoga muqabil kisi ka faiz[12]

[The sight of the renowned Nawab's attendant
   company,
It has the station of majesty, surpassing all beauty.
Was it Jamshed, the wretch, with the glitter of
   prosperity?
I would forego him for all that, my dear aunty!
The stores of luxury around his presence, let they be
   seen!
Even in his dreams Jamshed such as these would not
   have seen!

The revellers' bodies are draped in their finest raiments.
Finer than dressed silk appear to be their vestments.
Their waists adorned with watches like golden ornaments.
Loaded with gold, gold-thread-waisted are the boy-
   servants.

For all to witness are His Highness's generous favours,
What of Hatim, when no one can match such favours!]

In the manner of poems of praise in Persianate culture,
while Jan Sahib's poem does compare the earthly festival
with a heavenly parade, it is grounded in a secular, material
metaphor and not in a religious one. The qualities of the
princely ruler are manifested in vision of a generous Nawab
or ruler who provides patronage. The poem, therefore,
begins by invoking the royal patron before moving on to
a variety of actors, speech forms and subjects visible in the
festive marketplace.

In the lines quoted above, the overt tone is of the
lower-class woman speaker addressing an older woman in
her immediate domestic space. This is the conventional
mode of Rekhti speech and poetry written in it. As this
mode is used to describe the royal personage of the ruler
and his semi-divine properties, we should note here the
mixing of styles and social distinction within the body
of the Rekhti poem. This inevitably raises the question
of caste and labour, which are central to Jan Sahib's
ethnographic lens, in the making of a Muslim polity and
identity. A couple of examples of how the poet refers to
marginalized caste-cum-occupational groups such as the
washerman (*dhobi*), butcher (*qasa'i*), gardener (*mali*),
house steward (*khansaman*) and *kanjar* (people of 'low'

caste whose employment consists in making and selling strings, etc.) will illustrate the working of this lens. The definition of these terms in standard dictionaries like Platts shows the collapsing of labour and caste specifications in the verbal unity of the caste name. However, the caste connotation preponderates in the poetic-ethnography mode of Jan Sahib as he limns the occupational skills and artefacts made by the workers and artisans, displaying both class- and caste-related anxieties and even contempt within his poetic description. Consider the following stanza from the poem:[13]

a'in nikhar nikhar ke mahallon se bhanginen
jo rokta hai kehti hain mat tok re hame
panjon ke bal hain chalti dikha kar nazakaten
suthri hain jhaadutara si ghamze na kyun karen
jo ghoora unka pyara ko'i aane jane par
Goga ki qasmen khane lagin woh kamane par

[Scrubbed and clean the sweeperesses from their localities make an entry,
Should anyone accost them, they reply: 'Do not even try!'
They walk on display balancing on their toes, very spry.
If they're bright like a broom-star comet, why won't there be coquetry?

10

As they stride if some paramour dare cast a glance,
By Goga! Their god of latrine-cleaning, they address
  him askance.]

The diction of cleansing (*nikhar*) is associated with the caste-cum-occupational identity of the woman sweeper (*bhangin*). She is the labourer who cleans the streets and latrines, and, therefore, works with dirt. However, within the festival space, their presence is defined not just by their caste occupation, but also by a resistance that goes with their emergence in that space. They vocally resist those who thwart their spatial and market mobility. Thus, the gendered body and speech of the 'low-caste' woman becomes both a site of spectacle for popular consumption as well as a reinscription of her caste identity. While Urdu scholars have commented upon the gendered qualification of poetic discourse, especially in the ghazal, they have failed to give an account of the political economy of caste and labour in which it is embedded. Jan Sahib's ethnographic mode takes this economy for granted and through the poetic convention of metonymic elaboration (i.e., using metonymies of a single theme, here the 'cleaning' profession) shows the contrast between the special display of the sweeper women on the festival day and the everyday reality of their labour and its harsh conditions. The stanza that follows the one above states:

khush hain ubaal doodh ki surat hain la rahin
aur khatte mithe bol hain apne suna rahin
hain 'ishq ko to husn ka zaamin bana rahin
bala'i bala dil men hain naqshe jama rahin
mithi zuban dahi se siva aisi boli hai
jo bat ghosanon ki hai makkhan ki goli hai

[In high spirits they make a boiling milkiness.
As they let out cuss words half-tangy, half-sweetness.
While they raise desire with beauty's yeastiness,
They have designs on the heart's frothy creaminess.
Their sweetness of tongue exceeds their yogurt.
Like a dollop of butter is the milkmaid's argot.]

The usage of caste and occupation-related metonymies provides a social perspective on the question of space, its occupation by speech and the subjectivities that exist in it. The subaltern women's speech is marked by abusive words as well as 'yogurt-like' sweetness. The pleasure of the banter of the 'low' caste/class women is the bedrock of the flavour of 'women's speech' as celebrated in Urdu studies in the form of both Rekhti poetry and the mannered *begamati zuban* (the ladies' argot). This is a point overlooked in the studies on space, speech and subjectivity in existing scholarship.

Kumkum Sangari has raised the question of caste and knowledge production in Urdu literary culture. She observes that the literary space is particularly interesting as it marks the entry of 'lower'-caste and -class subjects in the time of social and cultural reformism characterizing the late nineteenth century in colonial South Asia. Sangari argues that within the literary sphere the identity of caste was reconfigured as an occupational category, well beyond any religious affiliation.[14] She shows the operation of this colonial–ethnographic logic in vernacular tales (*qissa*) in defining, in her example, the *bhatiyaran* (a woman inn-keeper), *bahrupiya* (mimic), *bhaand* (jester, buffoon, actor, mime, mimic, strolling player [usually Muslim]) and *nat* (a dancer, rope-dancer, tumbler, mime, actor, juggler, also the name of a particular vagrant caste).[15] We encounter here again the intersection of labour and caste categories in describing performative–occupational groups. The colonial–ethnographic state's attempts to institute the community-based demarcation between Hindu and Muslim in a pre-existing complicated identity matrix are no less pertinent here. The question here is not just of a fixed religious identity and communal boundaries, but also the intersection of a politics of prejudice and of demarcating 'lower' castes and their labour that marks the poetic-ethnography mode. Colonial and vernacular forms of knowledge, therefore, were deeply entangled and implicated in producing knowledge claims about caste; indeed, their major articulation happened through that means. The anxiety for an upturned social order in the potentially socially subversive space of the festival and the market is displayed clearly in literary writing, already evident from the eighteenth-century *shahrashob* poetry in Urdu and Persian which lamented the city's decline and the rise of 'lower' castes and classes. It is also evident in Jan Sahib's own writings and his *Musaddas* under discussion.[16]

In the stanza below, the poetic description potentially undermines, if not subverts, caste hierarchies in the shared space of the market and its music:

dhobi qasa'i saqqe to hain khand ga rahe
aur rajput apna hain aalha suna rahe
ik simt hain dafali rabana baja rahe
kunjre qasa'iyon ko hain woh bhi rijha rahe
Salar aur Madar ki ta'rif gate hain
Baley miyan ke nam pe bas lote jate hain

[Washerman, butcher and water-bearer in Awadhi are
    singing,
While their epic called Aalha the Rajputs are reciting.
On one side the drummers their tambourines are beating,
The lowest of the low, butchers and grocers, are they
    entertaining.
They sing songs for their deities, Salar and Madar, in
    devotion,

14

And roll about taking the name of Master Baley in
adoration.]

The stanza offers a particularly acute perspective to think
about caste, labour and linguistic usage within the shared
space of the marketplace. The mixing and collapsing of
spatial, linguistic and emotional registers are particularly
interesting. Not only are varieties of speech and musical
performance taken note of, but they all also combine in a
hybrid social formation connected in devotion to local Sufi
figures such as Salar of Ghazipur and Baley *miyan* of Meerut.
Thus, local musical and Sufi traditions create hybrid
communities of belief based in musical performance. We
suggest that Urdu literary history cannot be fully explained
without engaging and addressing the triad of labour, caste
and gender within the precincts of the bazaar economy.
We will return to this point later, but, for now, we can
proceed to map the literary landscape of the marketplace.

Women, Men and Transvestites

The fear of the marketplace encapsulates the fear of the
breakdown of spatial demarcations not just along class and
caste lines, but also along gender and language difference.
Rekhti has so far been largely examined and utilized to
understand women's domestic or inner emotional and

erotic domains. Jan Sahib creatively uses Rekhti here to talk about not just the female body and speech, but the body and speech as performative categories in the marketplace as well. It is here that his understanding and deployment of Rekhti should be viewed as a bodily and vocal transvestism, both as occasional masquerade and a discursive–performative act. In his poetic-ethnography mode, the poet describes all kinds of performing bodies present at the market. The most sought after being the women of the marketplace:[17]

apna javab rakhti nahin aaj nauratan
gana gala surila nihayat hi khush chalan
randi hai batamiz nahin jhut yeh sukhan
jo ta'ifa hai gul hai jagah unki hai chaman
bulbul ka bagh hota hai dil gul ke saamne
yeh gul shagufta hote hain bulbul ke saamne[18]

[Today Nauratan ensures that she remains peerless.
A sweet-singing voice, and tuneful no less.
A cultured whore she is and to declare it is not meaningless.
Each dancing girl a rose, belongs to the garden, no less.
Seeing the rose makes it a garden, the heart of the nightingale.
These flowers also decide to blossom to the song of the nightingale.]

First, we are introduced to the courtesan Nauratan, whose name literally means the nine jewels. The ornamental title of her name matches the quality of her melodious throat and her cultured manners. Her speech embodies her subjecthood even though she is referred to as a 'whore' (*randi*). She distinguishes herself through her voice and melodious singing supplemented by her charming manners. The Persianate metaphor of the nightingale (*bulbul*) in the garden (*chaman*) carries the weight of her self-presentation and subjecthood. The poem then proceeds to describe other courtesans at the festival:

> *hain apne dono kasb men suthri bahut nafis*
> *das hissa yeh zyada hain sab ta'ifon men bis*
> *Shirin se bhi zubanen rakhti hain salis*
> *har dil 'aziz kyun na hon kyun kar na hon anis*
> *badr-e-munir ek hai ik benazir hai*
> *maddah Mammi Chunno ka ek ek amir hai*[19]

[In their jobs both are polished and perform exquisitely.

Among dancing-girls, they are more than ten times twenty.

Sweeter than Shirin's, their speech is unfussy.

Why won't they be dear to every heart and be friendly?

The one 'Night-dispelling Moon', the other 'Incomparable',

17

Devoted to Mammi–Chunno is every patron and
   noble.]

Subba se deredar ki hain dono betiyan
ta'rif Mammi Chunno ki kya kijiye bayan
qabil yeh hain ra'ison' ki suhbat ke randiyan
jaisi hai Allahrakkhi zamane ko hai 'ayan
apne mizaj tinon amirana rakhti hain
Indar ki tarah ghar ko parikhana rakhti hain

[They are daughters of Subba and a wealthy courtesan—
To give the only description of Mammi and Chunno
   we can.
Women they are fit for soirees of any nobleman,
Just as Allahrakkhi is known to any worldly man.
All three of them an aristocratic way of life maintain,
Just like Indra's fairy house their house they maintain.]

Among the group of courtesans–performers are Mammi
and Chunno, both distinguished by their sweet speech
(*zuban*) which is the identity of their profession (*kasbi*).
Their linguistic–subjective identity is also institutionalized
in their occupation of a precise station in the marketplace.
These are courtesans with their own establishments
(*deredar tawa'if*). Based on their manners and the nature
of their establishment, they provide the social sites for

cultivated companionship to the elite men. Jan Sahib makes distinctions in the idiom to connote their appearance (*sarapa*) and the affective and sexual labour they provide. Thus, *deredar* (those having a fixed abode, i.e., are well-to-do) courtesans were distinguished from other market-women through the refinement of their manners (*batamiz, tahzib, sha'istagi*) and their involvement in singing, dancing and poetry writing, and not just sex work. The refined quality and elite (*amirana*) lifestyle of the aristocratic salon household (*parikhana*) of the deredar tawa'if separates the latter from the others in the marketplace, like the ones described in the following stanzas:

> *pandit hansor kahta bajakar yeh taali hai*
> *waqif nahin hun gori hai ya shakl kaali hai*
> *sharmati uske naach se Barmaan ki saali hai*
> *jadu ki pudiya Nanhi yeh Kalkatta waali hai*
> *hai khemta bhi jaanti par nachti nahin*
> *purab ka ko'i nach idhar nachti nahin*[20]

[With a loud clap he announces, that master of ribaldry:
'I am not aware whether she is fair or dusky.
Brahma's sister-in-law shies away in envy,
A magic lamp from Calcutta is our very own Nanhi.
She knows how to grind her hips but refuses to dance,
What she performs here is not just some eastern dance.']

sarkar hai yeh Hind ke Yusuf ki aashkar
kyun kar na ho 'aziz 'Azizan ka iftikhar
isko 'ata hua hai Zuleikha sifat waqar
hai is chaman men Misr ke bazar ki bahar
'Abbasi apna rang judagaana rakhti hai
har gul ko apna shefta diwana rakhti hai[21]

[Hers is the reign of the Indian Joseph, veritable.
How could 'Azizan's glory then not be admirable?
Bestowed on her a station, with Zuleikha equatable.
Garden and spring in the Egyptian bazaar are now
      comparable.
'Abbasi keeps her colours all distinguished,
Every flower she keeps in frenzy and anguished.]

hazir jawab randi 'ajab shokh o shang hai
Hingan bhi Lakhna'u ki pari sabza rang hai
joban hai naujavani ka dil men umang hai
alladpane [sic] *ke rakhti nirale woh dhang hai*
par Bandi Jan uski bahut baatamiz hai
khu bu mizaj jiska har ik ko 'aziz hai[22]

[The quick-witted wench is brazenly flirty,
Hingan of Lucknow, she too is a 'green fairy'.
Her breasts are youthful, her heart full of intensity.
She maintains her unique style of immaturity.

But her Bandi Jan shows great cultivation:
Her habits and comportment have universal
   admiration.]

un par karam ho mere Sulaiman ka sada
khaliq ne jinko martaba Bilqis ka diya
ghilmaan huren nachne gane pe hain fida
Darogha sahiba hain woh zi-rutba ai buwa
mangla mukhi hun dena du'a mera kaam hai
arbab men nishaat ki 'Bi Jaan' naam hai[23]

[May they remain blessed by Solomon forever!
They, whom the creator has deemed to have Bilqis's
   stature!
The paradisal boys and virgins, witnessing their arts,
   surrender,
Madame Darogha holds a high station, my dear
   aunty!
I, a dancing-girl, my calling is to spread cheer:
My name 'Bi Jaan' is well-known to any connoisseur.]

In this poetic-ethnographic description of the women of
the marketplace, we have dancers like Nanhi of Calcutta
who is known for her adept knowledge of a distinct
regional song-and-dance style (*khemta*) popular in
Calcutta. Hingan from Lucknow is known for her fairy-

like beauty (*pari sabza rang*) and others like Zuleikha and 'Azizan who trade their bodies are said to bring about the spring season (*bazar ki bahar*), beautiful but transitory, to the market.[24] Bandi Jan, even though a maiden, is known for her manners while the courtesan Darogha possesses much power due to her role and services at the palace. Finally, Bi Jaan acquired much name and fame among the connoisseurs of music and dance in the Rampur state.

We have some information from another text on the festival which devotes an entire section on the tawa'ifs or courtesans providing personal details about the various figures we encountered above, including Darogha Mahbub Jan who was apparently a close confidante of the Nawab not just during the fair, as he took her along with him for the pilgrimage to Mecca.[25] Lazzat Bakhsh tawa'if, who originally belonged to Lucknow, was employed in Rampur because of her singing talent.[26] Allahrakkhi was also from Rampur and was known for her singing and her hobby of keeping chickens which earned her the nickname 'the chicken' (*murghi*). Nanhi Kalkatte-*wali* was not from Rampur but came to perform there at the festival every year. 'Abbasi was from Rampur and was known for her happy nature.[27] While 'Azizan could both sing and dance. Hingan Jan who came from Rampur was employed by the government and subsequently at the Bilsi court and was renowned for her singing. Bandi Jan too was employed by the Rampur state.[28]

Each of these figures of the marketplace is connected and separated from one another based on speech and a spatial identity which allows us to map the complex and changing landscape of courtesans and their trade in the post-1857 period. Some were successful while many were turned into one other commodity in the semi-colonial market of the princely state. This turn in fortunes is marked in the diction of Jan Sahib's poetry:

> *phulon ke haar hathon ke hain gajre badhiyan*
> *bedamon bechte hain inhen le ko'i miyan*
> *shauqin mard lete hain shauqin randiyan*
> *mali bhi malinen bhi yahi karti hain bayan*
> *albeli aao lo yeh palang tod bela hai*
> *Dilli ke phulwalon se behtar yeh mela hai*[29]

[Flower garlands and flower bracelets ready to tie,
Sold at no price if only some gentleman would buy.
Enthusiast women for enthusiast men to buy.
Thus, even the gardeners and their wives specify:
'Girl! Come take these bed-breaking, love-making jasmine flowers.
This fest does not compare with Delhi's parade of flowers.']

The changing political economy after the 1857 turmoil undermined traditional patronage structures and sharpened, if not created, the caste and class hierarchies (deredar tawa'if, *mujrewali*, *raqqasa*, randi, *kasbi*, *kanjri*) among market-women whose work profile ranged from affective–cultural labour to sex work. In this poetic ethnography, we glimpse the entire range of actors within the category of 'market women'. These range from established courtesans, those who moved to the princely state's entertainment departments, to those who travelled across cities from colonial Calcutta to princely Rampur or those who were scrounging for their existence after the 1857 debacle in the marketplace. The festival provided refuge and patronage and compared favourably with the pre-1857 Mughal flower-festival of Delhi. These women were not alone in seeking princely patronage as the marketplace of labouring bodies was full of male, female and transvestite performing bodies. It is to these other categories of performers that we now turn.

Apart from the women's sphere, there is the disruptive world of vernacular-gendered performance styles consisting of the male *ta'ifa* (dancer), randi (whore), *zanane* (effeminate), *hijda* (eunuch), bhaand (jester) and *rekhti-go* (Rekhti performer), including Jan Sahib himself, who are part of the transactions in the festive marketplace. He describes this other world through the qualities of the performance skills of these figures and puts himself in his own category as a purveyor of wordsmith skills.

> *pesh-e-nazar yeh rahta hai har aan ta'ifa*
> *mardaney ta'ifon men 'Ali Jan ta'ifa*
> *rakhta ziyada sab se hai yeh shaan ta'ifa*
> *is ta'ife pe aur ho qurban ta'ifa*
> *sarkar ko hamaare yihi bas hansata hai*
> *jo nakhrey uske sunta hai khud lot jata hai*[30]

[He remains forever in the mind among the boy-dancers.
'Ali Jan, *the* boy-dancer, among all boy-dancers.
In lustre he exceeds all the other boy-dancers.
In his place may be sacrificed all boy-dancers!
Only he manages to tickle our royal master,
Audiences of his tantrums double up with laughter.]

> *Nauroz Holi kijiye is jashn par nisar*
> *saqqe bhare hain rangon ki mashaken ka'i hazar*
> *shabbu se hain bana rahe har ek ko lala-zar*
> *kausar to hauz rang men jannat ki hai bahar*
> *mele ka taur turfa hai bas apne dhang par*
> *tasviren randi mardon ki hain ek rang par*[31]

[That Nauruz and Holi are sacrificed for our festival is
    a given.

Thousands of waterskins are colour-filled by watermen.
With the night-blooms they spray everyone tulip-crimson.
Kausar is but a pond, these colours are the flourish of
      heaven.
This variety of fair is only one of a kind,
Where girls and men are painted the same kind.]

Scholarship on courtesans has given an impression that it
was an all-female profession. However, in the marketplace
men too performed as dancers or ta'ifa. The most famous
of them, from the above stanza, was 'Ali Jan who apparently
was the Nawab's favourite not just because of his dancing
skills, but more crucially for his humorous verbal artistry and
camp performance (*nakhrey*). Apart from male dancers, there
were also male prostitutes (*mard* randi) of every possible hue
(*rang*). The metaphor of colour is particularly interesting as
it connects the physical world with ideal typologies, allowing
us to imagine a variety of subjectivities on a spectrum of
colours without centring on any category or personality. In
a commentary written on the text, another Rampuri scholar
provides insights into the personal histories of the performers
at the fair. He devotes, for example, an entire section on the
tawa'ifs. Interestingly, he does not include 'Ali Jan, the ta'ifa,
in the section but classes him under the 'remaining doyens
of music' (*baqaya arbab-e-mausiqi*) alongside *gawa'iyyas*
(songsters), *qawwals* (*qawwali* singers), pakhawaj and

shehnayi players such as 'Ali Jan Nachaniya whose home was Rampur and who was the husband of the dancing girl Jan Mirasan. Apparently, he did both—sang and danced.[32] However, the poet Jan Sahib does not shy away from using gendered performative categories for a range of other male bodies too. Consider the following stanza from the *Musaddas*:

bhatiyariyan kahin kahin ladte hain hijde
phakkad to hain zanane zananon se lar rahe
aur un men kuchh 'ata'i jugat rang marduwe
hain chhant-te ramuzen zila' bhi hain bolte
thatta hai tamashbinon ka thatte lagate hain
diwar-e-qahqaha ka namuna dikhate hain[33]

[Here, inn-keeper women bicker, there are the castrates,
While busy swapping insults are the effeminates.
And among them some wannabe poet laureates
Make double entendres, innuendoes and vulgar
     agglutinates.
All the revellers are in mood, making raucous revelry.
And like the great laughing wall of China, they are
     exemplary.]

gane bajane wale mulazim hain beshumar
khat raag itna kaun sunega hai ashkar
hain bhaand jo Bareli ke mashhur teen chaar

karte chithaar randiyon ki hain woh baar baar
ham unke uhi mujre men hazir jo hote hain
dariya men sharm ke hamen mauji dubote hain[34]

[Singers and musicians in employ are numberless.
How much can one listen to a 'sixth' raga endless?
Bareilly has three or four mimickers, more or less.
On the wenches they shower invectives countless.
As we assemble—oh my—to attend the entertainment:
The thrills drown us in a sea of utter amazement.]

Here is a world saturated with gendered performance and speech acts. The latter include the effeminates (zanane) engaged in vocal duels using rhymed invectives, transvestite performers (*hijde*) and mimes and mimics (*bhaand*) each of whom are noticeable by their peculiar self-presentation through speech. All of them are known for their rowdy performances and thus produce subversive yet pleasurable speech acts. The emotions arising, therefrom, range from laughter, embarrassment and shame. Higher up in the speech hierarchy are the legendary singers and poets.

Marketplace of Speech

Finally, a crucial aspect of the production of space in the poetic–ethnographic mode is the relation between speech and identity. This comes alive in the discussions on poets, storytellers and reciters of elegy and gender-crossing poetry (*dastan-go, marsiya-go, rekhti-go*) in the poem, each of whom is identified with their art. Jan Sahib interestingly discusses them together in a section of their own. From these examples, a general proposition can be offered that the marketplace is a site of competing speech forms and, therefore, subjectivity formation. Taking note of this performative aspect of his poetic ethnography mode and documenting in the Rekhti-style, Jan Sahib himself occupies a gender-bending voice as he plays with the embodiments of gender. This allows him to elaborate upon the diversity of speech and subjectivities present at the festival. It is to the diversity of speech and their concomitant subjectivities that I now turn.

> *har shab ko nau baje dar-e-daulat pe aate hain*
> *har roz shadiyana khushi ka bajate hain*
> *har roz lal parde pe shahana gaate hain*
> *har roz ho ke surkh-ru sabko rijhate hain*
> *shahna-nawaz Mir 'Ali jis ka naam hai*
> *raushan hai uski chauki yeh mah-e-tamam hai*[35]

[At nine, at the gilded door in the evening every day,
They play melodies of happiness every day.
Before the durbar's red curtain, they sing the *shahana*
     every day.

They lure all and one unabashedly every day.
Mir 'Ali is the name of the *shehnayi* maestro.
The full moon is he; around him the dais is aglow.]

Asghar 'Ali Hakim woh hain dastan-go
Ahmad 'Ali se kam nahin Qasim 'Ali se jo
hain Lakhna'u ke charb-zuban vuhi kyun na ho
Sayyid 'Ali bhi fard hain is fan men aj to
jhartey hain phul munh se 'ajab khush-zuban hain
bulbul ki tarah kahte sadaa dastan hain

[Asghar 'Ali Hakeem happens to be a tale-teller.
Ahmad 'Ali or Qasim 'Ali, he is not less than them or
    better.
He comes from Lucknow, so won't he be a smooth
    talker!
Today Sayyid 'Ali, too, in this art form is getting better.
Petals drop from his mouth; he is unique in oratory.
Like a nightingale he always delivers the story.]

do dastan-goyon ne yeh baat ki na'i
kya khub dastan kahi dhum-dham ki
do roz main bhi sun-ne ko ai begaman ga'i
suhbat yahi chaman men 'ajab benazir thi
Hamza ki hai qasam kahi 'ayyari Mir ne
yeh dekha bazm loot li lo sari Mir ne[36]

Introduction

[Two storytellers have done something new:
They have composed a yarn that consists of much ado.
I too went to listen, ladies, the day before or two:
The company at the garden was incomparable too.
Upon Hamza, I swear, Mir's speech was pure artistry.
The entire audience was floored by Mir's spell of
    mystery.]

Munshi ne 'ishq woh kaha bashshash ho ga'i
sun-sun ke uski garmiyan aubash ho ga'i
joban dhalaa za'if main hun kaas ho ga'i
lekin siva javanon se 'ayyash ho ga'i
yeh pasta-qad hai qahar ka 'afat ka marduwa
yeh dastan-go hai qiyamat ka marduwa

[The Munshi told a love story which left me elated.
Listening to its steamy scenes I felt excited and titillated,
Youth then declined, like old grass I was decimated.
Yet much more than a youngster I became agitated.
This short-statured but sensational, stupendous fellow,
A storyteller to end all storytellers, is this fellow.]

duniya men uhi bachey na hon kyun woh nek-kho
Mahdi ka jo ghulam Raza ka ghulam ho
ustad khushnavis hai ik dastan-go
nassar be-badal ko'i sha'ir hai dekh lo

31

yeh charon fan bane isi ustad ke liye
zeba yeh fan hain Ambahi Parshad ke liye[37]

[Well, there is still a person in the world who is pleasant:
A servant of the Mahdi is also Raza's servant.
A master calligrapher, he is a storyteller-savant.
No poet to substitute this prosaist, so say the observant.
They were made for this master, all the four arts.
For Ambahi Parshad they are better, all the four arts.]

mashhur sha'iron men hain Munshi Miyan Ameer
ustad jinke Munshi Muzaffar 'Ali Aseer
sha'ir Jalal aur Zaki donon benazir
yeh charon aftab hain charon mah-e-munir
sarkar is ruba'i ki tauqir karte hain
qit'e qasidey roz yeh tahrir kartey hain[38]

[Famous among the poets is the gentleman Munshi
     Ameer,
Whose teacher is Munshi Muzaffar 'Ali Aseer.
Jalal and Zaki are poets without a peer.
The four are the sun, all four the complete lunar sphere.
His Highness holds this quartet in very high esteem.
As they write verses and odes in a steady stream.]

karinda khair-khwah nihayat namak halal

darbar me Wazir 'Ali Khan hain bemisal
yeh 'aql ke hain badr rasaa zihn hai kamal
aaghaaz men hi rakhte hain anjaam ka khayal
mashhur khansaman hain naukar qadim ke
navvab-e-namdar bahadur karim ke

[A solicitous and utterly loyal official,
At the durbar, Wazir 'Ali Khan is incomparable.
A full moon of intelligence, his intellect a parable,
Before acting he keeps in mind the foreseeable.
A well-known custodian of the royal house, an ancient
    employee,
Belonging to our brave and illustrious, benevolent
    grandee.]

meri majaal kya hai jo kul ki likhun sana
sarkar ne hai kaam bhi un ko 'ata kiya
Dilli ke sha'iron men hain Navvab Mirza
roshan-dimagh nur ka gehna hai, ai buwa
kartey ghazal men apna takhallus woh Dagh hain
yeh sha'iron ki bazm men raushan chiragh hain[39]

[Who am I to write the praises of 'totality'?
His Highness has conferred on him his bounty.
Nawab Mirza is among the poets from Delhi,
An enlightened mind, an ornament of light, aunty!

He uses the pseudonym 'the scar' in his ghazal:
At the poets' assembly, he is a shining lamp veritable.]

yeh qadrdan ra'is salamat rahe mudam
dargah men khuda ki yahi unka hai kalam
jin ka ki Banu Mir Mujaavir 'Ali hai naam
mirza'i jama khane ka naam-e-khuda hai kaam
chhote bare khavas havale unhi ke hain
karte hamesha kaam woh sad aafirin ke hain[40]

[That connoisseur noble, may he live an eternity—
This is his prayer in God's sanctuary.
Whose name is the scion of Mir Mujaavir 'Ali.
A steward of the royal chamber, his vocation: meditating
    on divinity.
For the small and great nobility, he is the one responsible.
He always performs deeds a hundred times applaudable.]

kahti hai tab'a tul na de kar tu ikhtisar
ya rabb rahe hamesha yeh sarkar barqarar
ek ik vaheed-e-'asr hai yakta-e-rozgar
achchha hai achchhe marsiya-khvanon ka iftikhar
donon hain lajawab khushi gham ke ta'ife
bemisl soz-khwan muharram ke ta'ife[41]

[Intelligence says, do not lengthen but abbreviate;

O Lord, may this realm never vitiate!

Each and every man of his time is a consummate
laureate,

In the glory of the best elegy-reciters one cannot
differentiate.

Both companies of joy and melancholy are matchless.

The company of reciters of Muharram dirges is peerless.]

sarkar-e-zi-waqar ke iqbal ko sadaa
Allah de taraqqi yahi apni hai du'a
Wallah mela jashn ka kya khub hai huwa
Ai Jan kya majal miri jo karun sana
lakhon hi jalsey rah gaye mauzun na ho sakey
mauzun kisi tarah se woh mazmun na ho sakey[42]

[May the fortune of the reign of His Grand Majesty

Be improved by God—this be our only entreaty.

By God, this has been an excellent festive assembly!

O 'Jan'! What powers do you have to write its eulogy?

A million events remain which could not be versified,

Those themes, despite everything, remain unversified.]

Among the above-quoted poetic descriptions, poets are
described in a category of their own. This includes Ameer
Minai, Dagh Dihlavi, Jalal Lakhnavi and Mansoor. Apart
from the masters of Persian and Urdu poetry, we also

meet local *char bait* (quatrain) reciters who are present at the festival.[43] The survey of performers includes famous dastan-gos (storytellers): Hakim Asghar 'Ali, Mir Ahmad 'Ali, Qasim 'Ali, Mir Nawab, Sayyid 'Ali, Munshi Amba Parshad, Ghulam Mahdi and Ghulam Raza.[44] Through these passages, we come to know that the famous Rekhti composers moved from Lucknow and found refuge in Rampur where not only were they patronized but this dying art was also preserved through the nascent print culture and the Rampur library as well as the publication ventures of the Newal Kishore Press, Lucknow. A notable dastan-go in this context was Hakim Asghar 'Ali who was employed by Nawab Yusuf 'Ali Khan and contributed immensely to the preservation of the dastan-telling tradition in Rampur including Dastan *Tilism-e-hoshruba* and qissas like *Qissa roshan jamal*.[45] The inventory of performers and artists does not follow a modern sense of religious divisions. There were non-Muslim, proficient dastan-tellers such as Munshi Amba Parshad who was patronized by the Rampur Nawabs. Among his notable dastans are the *Dastan-e-sultana fitna*, and *Dastan-e-farrukh shahsavar*. Ghulam Mahdi also acquired a reputation as a dastan-go of Rampur. Another section of the poem maps the identity and artistry of the courtly musicians.[46]

The social observation of the poem's narrative trains itself on singers, storytellers, reciters of dirges and elegies, poets and eventually lands on Jan as the sole Rekhti poetry composer and reciter. In the festival space, all are competing to win favours and reputation through the mastery of speech and the emotions they can generate in patrons and audiences. Asghar 'Ali with his smooth Lucknow tongue, Sayyid 'Ali's reciting dastans like the fabled nightingale itself and Mir presenting his vocal artistry steal the show. There are nameless experts too such as the disciples of Ambahi Parshad who performed all kinds of popular dastans. Similarly, the unmatched marsiya-gos and *soz-khwan*s provide other forms of vocal artistry around a different set of emotions. Surrounded by all these speech acts and subjects is Jan Sahib himself as the last exemplary rekhti-go.

The organization of the text is interesting for it maps diverse speech acts and subjects in the topos of the festival. It starts with the praise of the Patron and ends at the Rekhti poet, Jan Sahib. In this movement from the patron to poet, Jan provides us with a range of speech acts and subjects limning the market space that has erupted around the festival. The constituents range from the princely elites, the service gentry, poets, performers and the subaltern classes. In this introduction, we have focused on the characteristics of space and speech, both performed and constructed within the market fair. We wish to highlight the creative usage of Rekhti to draw attention to not just the domestic but also the public sphere and wish to suggest that Rekhti is best seen as an innovation in South Asian literature where it interacted, gained and transformed a variety of living speech forms and subjectivities in distinctly vernacular locales.

Conclusion

In reflecting upon the histories of Islam and Muslims beyond the Arab world in a multicultural physical environment as well as among multilingual communities, the case of South Asia is crucial to map the histories of 'appropriation and domestication of local space and speech'. The Rekhti genre in Urdu is particularly revealing as it borrows from Indic, Deccani and North-Indian milieus to create hybrid speech forms and their related subjectivities. As conceptual historians, we must also enquire into the diverse vocabularies that constitute the language in which we think of the concept of Islam, whether in the primacy of Arabic or through the hegemony of English and other European languages. We must pay attention not just to the structure and final outcome, but also to the process of 'configuration of community' which, as debated among scholars, is linguistically and culturally determined and contingent and changing in nature. The relationship between Islam, space, speech acts and processes of integration should not merely be mapped in different regions, but one must also try to find what different definitions of Islam and the possibilities of being Muslim emerge in the process of linguistic and cultural transactions and not with the finished quality of a historical or social outcome.

Shahab Ahmed has written about the literary landscape of Islam that he calls the 'Balkan-to-Bengal complex'.[47] However, this trans-territorial category emerges only through the idea of circulation and shared aesthetics. But what about forms that do not travel or remain resolutely local? What might they teach us about locality, local speech and subjectivity? The Urdu language and the case of Muslims in India allow us a particularly interesting case to explore the limits of a trans-regional imaginary. Rampur was indeed connected to Bengal and the larger literary landscape that Ahmed refers to, but it imagined itself and circulated in decidedly local contexts, such as the Deccan, Delhi, Lucknow and Rampur. To rearticulate this in terms of a different debate: what are the genres, forms and subjectivities that appear and disappear in history and yet contribute in significant ways to the making of cosmopolitanism? We believe, the 'Balkan-to-Bengal complex' argument provides us with a layered structure that appears only too structured and well connected through literary genres. In fact, queerness in literature, for example, Rekhti, defies genre distinctions. It seems to me that Rekhti provides us with a far more complex world of speech forms and subjectivities limited neither to men nor women, but, in fact, works through a range of actors and subjectivities. In this case, Rekhti operates not just in the private realm but in the full glare of public view at a public festival as well. Speech, space and subjectivity are in a dynamic relationship here and it is this dynamism (and not complex) that merits further investigation. One might end by asking: What is *not* Islam? The capacity of Islam and Muslims to incorporate, integrate and elaborate on local traditions, speech forms and forms of subjectivity needs to be understood beyond a Balkan-to-Bengal complex and is better conceived of as a dynamic of the local and the translocal. Perhaps, it is this local cosmopolitan form of Islam that can claim to be truly global.

Translation

In the name of God, the merciful, the compassionate.

A poem in sestets to felicitate the festival of his gracious excellency, of exalted rank—the esteemed Nawab Kalb-e-Ali Khan—Hatim of the age, protector of the destitute, the enlightened presence, the ruler of Rampur—may his prosperity last forever!

[1]

Once more, as before, comes the renowned festival.
And witness, once more, the hubbub of the festival!
Once more, aunty, at the splendid full moon, a return
    of the festival.
Once more, in that incomparable garden, the crowds
    are at the festival.

Hear the warbling and the nightingale in every heart,
    once more!
The flower of joy is in bloom and a wondrous spring,
    once more.

[2]

Except at governance's door, crowds gather everywhere
    in this age.
All business is smoothly underway under the ruler's
    vassalage.
Those capable for a position are the ones put in charge,
And ready for the festivities is every equipage.
Hear all! The streets resound with preparations.
Everywhere the crowds speak of the artful vocations.

[3]

The who's who from England and Kashmir and far away,
Each one has his artistry on its fullest display,
And accept from the ruler wealth heaped on a tray.
I have witnessed all this: whoever knows, knows, okay?
You may search through the seven climes without success,
Yet the craft masters you meet here are simply peerless.

[4]

Craftsmen from all the world, the girls and the rakes,
    prominent,

Who shake the link chain between sky and firmament,
Travel from their cities and before His Highness are
    present.
Each one as famous in his art as a processional elephant!
The royal palace to their skill has been a witness.
The court of audience itself commends their greatness.

[5]

The new mansion at the royal court is just instituted—
The one called 'Mary among women', by God, is well-
    decorated!
Where only the English sahibs for breakfast are ever
    invited.
On two sides of the garden, canvases against walls are
    exhibited.
The Englishmen who come for a visit, O sirs, hear
    this—
All of London's parks and mansions no longer do they
    miss!

[6]

This festival, that in itself is a joyous festival,
Is agreeable to God; granted by God is this festival.
On display are wondrous creations during the festival.
The one who brings prosperity to people, it is *his*
    festival.

May God keep him protected on earth!
The festival's joys spread in heaven and on earth.

[7]

May God fulfil those whims—oh—in our heart, amen!
May his rank be higher than Solomon's, amen! Amen!
In the warrior's grip may the army remain unbeaten!
And as for his enemies may nary ever freshen!
These comely nobles are this land's ornament.
Beauty's grandeur, they are a majestic ornament.

[8]

Prosaists, calligraphers and the masters of recitation,
Perform their genres, to each his own pavilion.
When nothing's amiss, there's no room for exaggeration!
Language is remiss, the festival beggars all description.
Such a festive assembly to witness, witness our wonder
      now!
If this be a mirror, all faces are covered by sleeves now!

[9]

What may not have appeared even to an emperor,
At his presence's disposal are such things of pleasure.
The fire on Sinai may be compared to these lights'
      splendour.
God's creativity is made manifest here in Rampur.

They are like Moses's voice, these songs of the thousand-
voiced.

Why won't the festival bloom when springtime has
arrived?

[10]

The sight of the renowned Nawab's attendant
company,

It has the station of majesty, surpassing all beauty.

Was it Jamshed, the wretch, with the glitter of
prosperity?

I would forego him for all that, my dear aunty!

The stores of luxury around his presence, let they be
seen!

Even in dreams Jamshed such as these would not have
seen!

[11]

The revellers' bodies are draped in their finest raiments.

Finer than dressed silk appear to be their vestments.

Their waists adorned with watches like golden
ornaments.

Loaded with gold, gold-thread-waisted are the boy-
servants.

For all to witness are His Highness's generous favours,

What of Hatim, when no one can match such favours!

[12]

From the river Kosi for many *kos* only this manifested:

On foot everyone walks, while some riders are dismounted.

The canopies, awnings, marquees and tents cannot be counted.

Dew-catchers and a thousand pavilions in thousands are erected.

For the ladies-in-veils screened tents there are.

Such fine festival days, such fine nights they are.

[13]

Bunches of men gather around each budding mistress,

They ogle them and then puff up with happiness.

All hearts get pounded into the henna-hues of redness.

And the flirty ones extend their branches in flirtatiousness.

Each and every spectator of beauty enjoys the fruit.

A pretty face, verdurous, is every yearning's fruit.

[14]

Hey Champa, when I reach the festival and make an offering,

I will dress up as a gardener's wife, make a fruit-basket offering.

I will show my colours when the revelry is flowering.

A heap of marigolds on him, upon my life, will I be
    showering.
May he flourish and blossom, is my prayer for my master!
May he always revel in comfort, fingers crossed for my
    master!

[15]

The rose to the *keoda* flower thus addressed:
'What you say is true and remains unanswered.
A Joseph-faced nobility, he is, His Highness exalted.
A hundred yearnings arise, and youth is exceeded.
The valiant prince, our Nawab, the nameworthy,
By God's grace his age is between twenty-nine and
    thirty.'

[16]

Every blossom of the bud said, as it opened out:
'He's the lion of Muhammad, a friend of God, devout.
A seeker of yours, O my Ali, is what his name is about,
A just prince, Kalb-e-Ali Khan, a Hercules, no doubt!
Nauruz falls behind compared with today's festivity.
Blessed among all months is this month of felicity.'

[17]

That Nauruz and Holi are sacrificed for our festival is
    a given.

Thousands of waterskins are colour-filled by watermen.

With the night-blooms they spray everyone tulip-crimson.

Kausar is but a pond, these colours are the flourish of heaven.

This variety of fair is only one of a kind,

Where girls and men are painted the same kind.

[18]

The nightingale becomes a musician, and everywhere a garden.

The sweet-voiced cry in every nest, garden to garden.

Every heart's a blooming garden, every bed blooms in the garden.

Each bud carries gold in its fists in every flower garden.

O plumeria-coloured hyacinth! Your entanglements are now distant.

In place of the tulip's dark spot, look, its heart is effulgent!

[19]

'The flowers are no longer bud-less,' says the Indian jasmine.

'Whether plumeria, royal jasmine, "cupid's arrow" or double jasmine.'

'All bloom into a smile,' says the Arabian jasmine.

The lily's tongue says, 'Through the narcissus's eye,
   examine!'
What a rite of spring is at this festive assembly.
The chest heaves anew, what a unique festivity!

[20]

Why will the spring not enter the garden in bridal
   imitation?
It is the groom's day. May I be sacrificed for such
   celebration!
The winds of spring are coming, quick, at attention!
Said the little flower-footman, 'O high rider of flowers,
   pay attention:
May he remain humble, although the cockerel has a
   crest,
Let him know that in the garden he should be at rest.'

[21]

On the marigold's body the dress is all yellow
The spring dons a pre-wedding suit, unique and in
   yellow.
The greenery sways as the cool winds blow,
The dew is sprinkled not to let the dust blow.
A million colours in robes of all the flowers in bloom
This wondrous festival, the groomed guests and . . .
   here comes the groom!

[22]

To the red-ivy bride, true love is persistent:
'We belong to the festival, the festival our neck's ornament.
It is just for its sake that the meadow is verdant.
Our master's entry has made everyone look eminent.'
The versification of spring should happen in a flowery
    hand.
This theme's colour ought to be written by an adequate
    hand.

[23]

Flowers on earth and minds are puffed up to the sky.
    'Hark,'
says the east wind, 'everyone is verdant in the park.
Sparkling in their beauty are the tulips' dark mark.
In the garden, day and night, you and I are the burning
    spark.'
To the flower that blooms at night, the sun addresses:
'This park is watered with rose and *keoda* essences.'

[24]

Caretakers of relaxation are everywhere in arrangement.
Every wench and man drunk after their own manner of
    amusement.
Heaven may be too high but as if brought down in
    vanquishment,

In rank today the heavens lie on earth in debasement.
Such glitter flies today that earth resembles the sky.
The earthly particles give the impression of stars in the
    sky.

[25]

The spring is on display with many wondrous
    colourants.
The fair has stepped out in flowery accoutrements.
Even the mounties of the camel-riding artillery don
    colourful pigments.
And stationed on his chair is the captain of the
    regiments.
The sepoys swoon when the women players start
    singing,
Such gestures they make once their drums are
    drumming.

[26]

Many and everywhere are the confectioners' stalls.
Their shops, my darling date-cake, overflow with
    dough balls.
The poor sweets-seller cannot reach the end of his calls.
My darling barfi, overwhelmed is he by a thousand
    footfalls.
Even all the fleshpots of Egypt won't be so dandy.

Cat's got my tongue having polished off the sweets,
    dear candy.

[27]

The sweetmeat shops are where the sweet-styled are in
    a hustle.

Head-banging lovers no less than Farhad are in the
    jostle.

They don't speak much but, in their eyes, red threads
    nestle,

Like laddus they come in all sizes and many are in a
    bustle.

No room for a sesame seed, as they shout in all
    directions,

As if the sellers are falling dizzy selling sweet sesame
    confections.

[28]

Silver worth lakhs is flowing, their gold lakhs are
    spending.

In the wine-girls' hearts the seeds of friendship they're
    planting.

The melancholics of always begin loudly laughing,

A cloud of heavy smoke from the pipes they are
    smoking.

Each hemp-brown one is sieving hemp-leaf powder,

The wine-girl serves lightning, surging a current of
    power.

[29]

The wine-girl shouts, 'I will pound you with my pestle.
My companion is being pounded and it's not bearable.
I will turn you into vapour and you'll scamper in a
    tumble.
I do not mince words. I speak no ladylike vocable.
I have brought here all I looted of Lucknow's tokes.
When have I ever given a fig about these blokes?'

[30]

A wine-girl from Aminabad, to Rampur have I come.
I am the only one whom his presence considers
    welcome.
As for the others, on my appearance their allure has
    become—
The difference between hellfire and light, O sweet
    kingdom!
May he shower me with bounty every year and always!
The nameworthy Nawab may he survive always!

[31]

The train of us wine-girls will always be the rarest.
To the seat in the royal crimson pavilion we are nearest.

With hookahs made of gold and silver are we blest.
Sending blessings upon the rich, puff away the humblest.
We charge two gold coins for one fill of the hookah.
They come here to smoke, from the rajah to the fellah.

[32]

How well their stalls the moneychangers have decorated!
Gold and silver ornaments on sheets lie uncounted.
Without a fear of thieves, they are happily exhibited.
Heaps of rupee and gold coins lie everywhere deposited.
They are eager to raise loans of pice and cowries.
'Come!' they holler if you want to change your monies.

[33]

There the jewellers' shops are, about which here's the
    statement:
Weighing precious stones, Mr Ruby-Pearls makes an
    assessment.
Two brokers he has but their partnership causes some
    bafflement:
Emerald says to diamond, about our value how can
    there be agreement?
Madams Nose-Ring and Ruby some jewels have they
    bought.
With the munificence of His Highness, gratis have they
    got.

[34]

The drapers have their shops so well-carpeted,
That the satin sky observing them is impressed.
Such pieces of brocades and damask are on display
    spread!
And bundles of golden lace lie about unwrapped.
All the fairgoers, whether from near or far, declare:
Pieces of muslin embroidery spread around a glare.

[35]

The status of each retailer is told by his ware.
All his ware from home is brought here to the fair.
At throwaway rates, a fixed price is tagged nowhere.
He doesn't have to ask: how many would you care?
Well, when the nameworthy Nawab is recompensing,
What shopkeeper would not make a killing!

[36]

Abundance at no price is the fair's condition.
A player beg for alms? That is out of the question.
With a smile on their face, each player shows perfection.
The prince is a connoisseur and they're sure of his
    appreciation.
The wheel of heaven stops with their magical tricks,
Turning a hide into a cat, and other feather-into-a-
    pigeon tricks.

[37]

The festival takes on the air of the calendrical poem
ambient.

Carousels and swings of many colours are everywhere
salient.

A thousand-streamed fountain runs as if raining a
torrent.

Girls and men on swings sing out jubilant.

Predict, O Brahmin, when my man will stop
peregrinating?

Dresses are tinselled, and a spray of colour is raining.

[38]

Our festival's fair has made the Holi revels run aground.

Such entertainment the mimics have rehearsed to
astound:

A man on a hook and a rope, like a disc, going round,

The jugglers show their tricks which dumbfound.

Those who call out to Kali every time, sister dear,

These worshippers of hair are *Muslims*, sister dear!

[39]

Vendors with huge trays, and some small-tray vendors.

Clanking their cups everywhere are the water-sellers.

Over their pots of juice bent over are the juicers.

And barley-sugar candy are the real jawbreakers.

All the wares at the festival will not compare to a thing.
Fish kababs on skewers over frying pans are sizzling.

[40]

Opium-eaters gather where opium is cooking,
Sugarcane is peeled and parched-rice discs are frying.
The tongue tastes them and like fine silk they are
    melting,
But my temperament inclines to the cups of pudding.
Opium-eaters talk the same to poppy drinkers, saying
    things like:
'This lovely sweetmeat is marvellously tulip-like!'

[41]

I am crazy for one, but my beloveds are two!
Their gay temperament is sweeter than pudding, heigh-
    ho!
They turn into a kind heart anyone ill-disposed hitherto,
So why won't everyone want to get close to them too?
A man who shuns sweets and opium,
We do declare he is not bound for Elysium!

[42]

Sohan cake with nuts is being cooked somewhere near;
The colour of Persian almond sweets is its veneer,
While others say it is like a round block of paneer.

Paradise itself considers the sweet pearls-of-paradise
    dear.
The sellers declare at this festival extraordinaire:
These brilliant white pudding cups with the full moon
    do compare.

[43]

Flower garlands and flower bracelets ready to tie,
Sold at no price if only some gentleman would buy,
Enthusiast women for enthusiast men to buy.
Thus, even the gardeners and their wives specify:
'Girl! Come take these bed-breaking, love-making
    jasmine flowers.
This fest does not compare with Delhi's parade of
    flowers.'

[44]

Mongoose-and-snake fights staged by the snake-
    charmers,
And there bears are made to dance by their tamers.
Displaying their act on bamboo stilts are the rope-
    walkers.
And monkeys are made to ride goats by the monkey-
    keepers.
Women jugglers are showing their tricks in one corner.
Dressed in different characters appears the mimicker.

[45]

In one direction the puppeteers in a gathering plentiful,
On the tabla's beat they sing in Gujri tuneful
Twirling, a troupe of girly dancing boys, each graceful.
Singing ghazals on the beat, each boy so very graceful.
Their personae are ghouls, fairies and the crowned
    heads.
Their voices piercing, the trill of notes sharper than
    arrowheads.

[46]

All hearts are pierced by their affectionate archery.
Each heart and life sacrificed to their beauty and tuneful
    artistry.
The oglers announce to each other their plans of lechery:
'Let's pull them in a corner, the cute boys who do
    eyebrow-archery.'
No chance of leaving now that our hearts are shot.
May this festival last a year, we will enjoy it a lot!

[47]

Washerman, butcher and water-bearer in Awadhi are
    singing,
While their epic called Aalha the Rajputs are reciting.
On one side the drummers their tambourines are
    beating,

59

The lowest of the low, butchers and grocers, are they
    entertaining.
They sing songs for their deities, Salar and Madar, in
    devotion,
And roll about taking the name of Master Baley in
    adoration.

[48]

Here, inn-keeper women bicker, there are the castrates,
While busy swapping insults are the effeminates.
And among them some wannabe poet laureates
Make double entendres, innuendoes and vulgar
    agglutinates.
All the revellers are in mood, making raucous revelry.
And like the great laughing wall of China, they are
    exemplary.

[49]

Scrubbed and clean the sweeperesses from their localities
    make an entry,
Should anyone accost them, they reply: 'Do not even
    try!'
They walk on display balancing on their toes, very spry.
If they're bright like a broom-star comet, why won't
    there be coquetry?
As they stride if some paramour dare cast a glance,

By Goga! Their god of latrine-cleaning, they address
    him askance.

[50]

In high spirits they make a boiling milkiness.
As they let out cuss words half-tangy, half-sweetness.
While they raise desire with beauty's yeastiness,
They have designs on the heart's frothy creaminess.
Their sweetness of tongue exceeds their yogurt.
Like a dollop of butter is the milkmaid's argot.

[51]

And the greengrocer women have brought baskets of
    greenery,
Saucy natures they have and each one a green fairy.
Their breasts carry the weight of the oranges of beauty.
Each with a golden shine, each one without impurity.
They stand in the garden in a queue with full bosoms,
Spring has come to the fair, it appears, in their bosoms.

[52]

The sky says aloud that this is a festival most excellent.
From the rich to the poor there is a lot of merriment.
Brown-beauties at the fair with faces so piquant,
That heavenly boys, houris and angels are palpitant.
Young sirs many have come from a great distance,

As devotees of this festival, devoted to his presence.

[53]

Under the canopies everywhere are assemblies of song
and dance.

It is true, the greatest dancers are here in performance,

Which is why, aunty mine, Venus and Jupiter have lost
confidence.

The clappers the sound of thunder are poised to
outdistance.

The tabla-strike reaches high into the firmament.

Thunder is humbled at every beat's commencement.

[54]

Even on the musical scale, notes exceed their
measurement.

Every dancing woman's voice is quite resplendent.

Such trill of notes at which the organ is hardly
competent.

The black cuckoo also concedes that it is incompetent.

And the nightingale was lost when notes in the garden
it caught.

The ardour for the roses in its heart came to nought.

[55]

All musicians of note are employed by him.

They stand now with folded hands on one side before
    him.
They are summoned for His Majesty to perform for him.
Each one is a king cobra and none second to him.
They present dhrupads, tappas, khayals and melodies.
They consider Baiju and Tansen not even preliminaries.

[56]

The instrumentalists with the singers are beyond
    comparability.
I will now tell you of the musicians' names and their
    artistry:
When Baqir 'Ali the khayal singer presents a ditty,
Both Venus and Jupiter's orbits go into a tizzy.
The paradisal boys and houris are thrown into
    agitation,
If they catch the trills of this radiant vocalization.

[57]

The essence of musicality, they are all in his pay.
They steal the hearts of listeners in many a way.
But been players enchant with songs about lovers gone
    away,
That musk deer from Tartary come to listen from
    China all the way.
A wondrous spectacle here is of the Maker's potency.

The musicians' rostrum, sister dear, is a place of
   harmony.

[58]

Haidar, the sarangi player from Delhi, is how he is
   known.
Why won't he be the recipient of shawls from the well-
   known?
On the sarangi his hundred-coloured skill has he shown.
Undoubtedly, he has learned from maestros of renown.
At both the tabla and pakhawaj, Madhu shows mastery.
His hands perform like voice, such is his artistry!

[59]

Let us pray in every breath for our master's safety.
May we be taken in place of his great majesty!
Why won't we send him blessings when we enjoy his
   bounty?
And that each day be a festival, we recite this plenty.
The only refuge we have in the world is right here,
And Subba and Hassu Khan concur that it is right here.

[60]

When Allu and Mandru take to the platform.
They play the usual melodies but to the scale they don't
   conform.

Their love for song is such that they are always in form.
And we listen happily as they gayly perform.
One introduces a dhrupad, another vocalizes the
    percussion.
This musical stage has turned, O sir, into Indra's
    heavenly session.

[61]

Its inventor, O God, may his fame live forever.
An intelligence that made this instrument must be clever.
Its form is the sitar's, it has the sarangi's voice, however.
Like the sweet-voiced been its notes do not waver.
This alluring instrument Nanha does play best.
I vouch that he plays it better than all the rest.

[62]

Singers and musicians in employ are numberless.
How much can one listen to a 'sixth' raga endless?
Bareilly has three or four mimickers, more or less.
On the wenches they shower invectives countless.
As we assemble—oh my—to attend the entertainment:
The thrills drown us in a sea of utter amazement.

[63]

Incomparable are they today, among rabab players
    matchless,

That is why they have been selected by His Highness.
It befits them and therefore the awards of greatness.
The secrets of ragas and notes they know in truthfulness.
Listen all! Among string-players they are tsars.
They are the full moon, their epigones merely stars.

[64]

They really are descendants of Ustad Pyare Khan.
Thus, have I heard, sister-ladies, from the songstress'
    clan.
A leader of his art is Bahadur Husain Khan:
By God, his sursinghar and rabab recitals! Have mercy
    on man!
Only such attendants are worthy of appointment,
For our ruler is a connoisseur and they are transcendent.

[65]

Their throat is melodious, the voice a musical-note
    excavation.
They exceed Behzad in their mode of representation.
In the Deepak raga they bring about a picture's
    depiction.
Their song and their voice have an oceanic projection.
They are dhrupad and been players, but singers great
    too.
They sing very well even as they play well too.

[66]

The tongue shall fall short before their description.
It would elude too the poets of delicate versification.
Such slender knots they tie in their scale's composition,
That their song, throughout the world, holds
    distinction.
Such voices are rare among the thousands that sing.
In their every stretch of notes, a threaded pearl string.

[67]

The masters of qawwali present their incomparable skill,
And the lotus heart blooms just listening to them trill.
A stony heart melts like wax at their well-timed trill:
Restlessness becomes restless, it does not become still.
His name, Kazim Ali, and his title is 'the maestro'.
The beauty of his singing is most proper, right ho!

[68]

Among the maestros Murad Ali Khan had no succession.
His singing was renowned, the khayal his genre of
    composition.
Every person knew him to be a master of perfection.
His performances at Lucknow elude all description.
When his art matured, he had advanced into seniority.
Although still awake, in a long slumber lies his prosperity.

[69]

Among the dancing-girls of our time, 'the Egyptian' is
    important:
If her name is Lazzat, her song is bound to be piquant!
Her sweet tongue is tastier than the sweetest fondant.
Her song is made of sugar, her voice buttery unguent.
Among self-immolant lovers she is known to be light-
    hearted.
Her perfection in the profession is very well reported.

[70]

Today Nauratan ensures that she remains peerless.
A sweet-singing voice, and tuneful no less.
A cultured whore she is and to declare it is not
    meaningless.
Each dancing-girl a rose, belongs to the garden, no less.
Seeing the rose makes it a garden, the heart of the
    nightingale.
These flowers also decide to blossom to the song of the
    nightingale.

[71]

In their jobs both are polished and perform exquisitely.
Among dancing-girls, they are more than ten times
    twenty.
Sweeter than Shirin's, their speech is unfussy.

Why won't they be dear to every heart and be friendly?
The one 'Night-dispelling Moon', the other
    'Incomparable',
Devoted to Mammi–Chunno is every patron and noble.

[72]

They are daughters of Subba and a wealthy courtesan—
To give the only description of Mammi and Chunno
    we can.
Women they are fit for soirees of any nobleman,
Just as Allahrakkhi is known to any worldly man.
All three of them an aristocratic way of life maintain,
Just like Indra's fairy house their house they maintain.

[73]

With a loud clap he announces, that master of ribaldry:
'I am not aware whether she is fair or dusky.
Brahma's sister-in-law shies away in envy,
A magic lamp from Calcutta is our very own Nanhi.
She knows how to grind her hips but refuses to dance,
What she performs here is not just some eastern dance.'

[74]

Those who arrange the musicians' rostrum with decorum,
Why won't his name, Rahimullah 'Sarparast', be
    famous in the kingdom?

It is he who lends revelry to the musicians' rostrum.

May his rank remain high, may it fall not a modicum.

May His Highness's graciousness be upon all, ladies
and gents,

And no one should vainly boast of their accomplishments!

[75]

Considered the cuckoo and the nightingale of their
guild.

What a throat and palate especially when their notes
are trilled!

Cheek by jowl as they sing duets, the audiences are
thrilled.

As the world's most famous dirge reciters they are billed.

So qualified that each of their qualities makes pride
swell.

Both brothers are adepts—the world knows it very well.

[76]

A hail of stones on the chest of that acrobat, the bravest,

He who gets a slab of twenty maunds broken on his
chest.

Another lifted an entire camel—I was there, I do attest!

As if his strength drew on two entire millstones at its
best.

The acrobats were rewarded and recruited on duty.

If one skill is agreeable, all faults are forgotten, aunty!

[77]

Hers is the reign of the Indian Joseph, veritable.
How could 'Azizan's glory then not be admirable?
Bestowed on her a station with Zulekha equatable.
Garden and spring in the Egyptian bazaar are now
    comparable.
'Abbasi keeps her colours all distinguished,
Every flower she keeps in frenzy and anguished.

[78]

The quick-witted wench is brazenly flirty,
Hingan of Lucknow, she too is a 'green fairy'.
Her breasts are youthful, her heart full of intensity.
She maintains her unique style of immaturity.
But her Bandi Jan shows great cultivation:
Her habits and comportment have universal admiration.

[79]

He remains forever in the mind among the boy-dancers,
'Ali Jan, *the* boy-dancer, among all boy-dancers.
In lustre he exceeds all the other boy-dancers,
In his place may be sacrificed all boy-dancers!
Only he manages to tickle our royal master,
Audiences of his tantrums double up with laughter.

[80]

At nine, at the gilded door in the evening every day,
They play melodies of happiness every day.
Before the durbar's red curtain, they sing the *shahana*
    every day.
They lure all and one unabashedly every day.
Mir 'Ali is the name of the shehnayi maestro.
The full moon is he, around him the dais is aglow.

[81]

Asghar 'Ali Hakeem happens to be a tale-teller.
Ahmad 'Ali or Qasim 'Ali, he is not less than them or
    better.
He comes from Lucknow, so won't he be a smooth
    talker!
Today Sayyid 'Ali, too, in this art form is getting better.
Petals drop from his mouth; he is unique in oratory.
Like a nightingale he always delivers the story.

[82]

Two storytellers have done something new:
They have composed a yarn that consists of much ado.
I too went to listen, ladies, the day before or two:
The company at the garden was incomparable too.
Upon Hamza, I swear, Mir's speech was pure artistry.
The entire audience was floored by Mir's spell of mystery.

[83]

The Munshi told a love story which left me elated.

Listening to its steamy scenes I felt excited and titillated,

Youth then declined, like old grass I was decimated.

Yet much more than a youngster I became agitated.

This short-statured but sensational, stupendous fellow,

A storyteller to end all storytellers is this fellow.

[84]

Well, there is still a person in the world who is pleasant:

A servant of the Mahdi is also Raza's servant.

A master calligrapher, he is a storyteller-savant.

No poet to substitute this prosaist, so say the observant.

They were made for this master, all the four arts.

For Ambahi Parshad they are better, all the four arts.

[85]

A complete compendium of artists is this list.

Before His Highness it becomes a courtiers' list,

Who declares it a list of feats to interrupt an endless list.

It is easy to listen, but Herculean to reach the end of
    the list.

I will read the list of names very slowly and lispingly.

The Nawab, worthy of his name, will reward me
    handsomely.

[86]

The honourable penmen whether great or ordinary.

Intelligent like the angel, they are all-knowing,
exemplary.

If titles are bestowed on them by His Grand Majesty,

It befits them, by God, may they ever be happy!

Did Akbar ever have such intellectual men?

He may have had the 'nine jewels', but not such perfect
men.

[87]

The dignity of the lawyers of His Highness is obvious.

They walk on the ground of intelligence and under the
sky sagacious.

O you, intelligent girl of mine, make the description
punctilious!

A quill they are in writing, in speech they are
loquacious.

Dear sirs, their renown has even spread to London.

They follow absolutely the prince's every instruction.

[88]

Famous among the poets is the gentleman Munshi
Ameer,

Whose teacher is Munshi Muzaffar 'Ali Aseer.

Jalal and Zaki are poets without a peer.

The four are the sun, all four the complete lunar sphere.

His Highness holds this quartet in very high esteem.

As they write verses and odes in a steady stream.

[89]

A solicitous and utterly loyal official,

At the durbar, Wazir 'Ali Khan is incomparable.

A full moon of intelligence, his intellect a parable,

Before acting he keeps in mind the foreseeable.

A well-known custodian of the royal house, an ancient
    employee,

Belonging to our brave and illustrious, benevolent
    grandee.

[90]

Who am I to write the praises of 'totality'?

His Highness has conferred on him this bounty.

Nawab Mirza is among the poets from Delhi:

An enlightened mind, an ornament of light, aunty!

He uses the pseudonym 'the scar' in his ghazal:

At the poets' assembly, he is a shining lamp veritable.

[91]

That connoisseur noble, may he live an eternity—

This is his prayer in God's sanctuary.

Whose name is the scion of Mir Mujaavir 'Ali.

A steward of the royal chamber, his vocation: meditating
    on divinity.
For the small and great nobility, he is the one
    responsible.
He always performs deeds a hundred times applaudable.

[92]

I have seen it a million times with my own eyes.
By God, I promise, I never ever tell lies.
All the gatekeepers included and even the lackeys,
Sayyid Fida 'Ali over them has power to scrutinize.
Sister dear, mummy dear, even they are in high standing,
The men whose job is to read letters to the king.

[93]

Once again the evening assembly begins, the festivity
    being over.
No one shall forget it, mark my words, for the entire
    year.
The garden is paradisal, milk flows through the river.
The charm of heaven's throne is in the palace's pure
    grandeur.
The river has the freshness of the Kausar and nectar
    streams.
In each of its waves a hundred oceans of goodness, it
    seems.

[94]

The light on the river is everywhere scattered;

They faint like Moses, from the light they have witnessed.

'From a blessed wilderness into the garden we have
     arrived,'

Standing on the riverbanks, the trees have thus uttered.

'I am the river extraordinaire, a current of existence.

May the pleasure-bathers give this young maid's words
     credence!'

[95]

The barge addressed the stream thus: 'O stream, listen
     to me:

This rank have I received from the feet of His Majesty.

I am Noah's ark, I am a vessel of delivery.

If Elias and Khizr row me, no wonder that it should be!

I am the venue for the festivity of His Highness
     Kalb-e-Ali Khan

It is the Rampur prince's festival, Solomon's festivity
     no less than!'

[96]

On the birthday every year of his great eminence,

A banquet takes place where light is in attendance.

The world entire is present, from around here and a
     great distance:

Some denizens of Lucknow, and some of Kanpur
    residence.
I lay my life down for my prince and his pomp and
    display:
All of Rampur has experienced the world as if in a play.

[97]

The graceful cap on his head, as if by Solomon crowned.
By God's grace today is the day of the royal festival
    renowned.
The senses declare that we are by Kalb-e-Ali Khan
    governed.
The festivity, its meed, from joy itself, has earned.
The artists-entertainers queue up to receive their handout.
The valiant Nawab, worthy of his name, is handing
    them out.

[98]

Those whose names are chosen for the roster of rewards,
They are the rarest among the courtiers and the royal
    wards.
Present in the presence of his presence are all the lords.
They are admitted to an intimate private audience
    afterwards.
Their faces glitter with gold-dust, their lucks are now
    shiny.

They are those whom the stars would blink at with
    envy.

[99]

May they remain blessed by Solomon forever!
They, whom the creator has deemed to have Bilquis's
    stature!
The paradisal boys and virgins, witnessing their arts,
    surrender,
Madame Darogha holds a high station, my dear elder
    sister!
I, a dancing-girl, my calling is to spread cheer:
'Bi Jaan' is my name, well-known to any connoisseur.

[100]

Intelligence says, do not lengthen but abbreviate:
O Lord, may this realm never vitiate!
Each and every man of his time is a consummate laureate:
In the glory of the best elegy-reciters one cannot
    differentiate.
Both companies of joy and melancholy are matchless.
The company of reciters of Muharram dirges is peerless.

[101]

The foundation of the Ka'ba lasts until one day,
The drumbeat of the faith sounds until one day,

May this festive fair remain, O God, till that day!

May the worthy Nawab of his name in all comfort stay!

Whatever I've chattered, may it be accepted as my labour!

The price of salt is paid, may prosperity be in my favour!

[102]

Good, bad, rotten, whatever was in store,

All was sold in the gathering, everyone richer than before.

Every consummate person was appreciated on this score.

This year's celebration was better than the year before.

Rampur is well-known, more than any major city.

The wedding festivities may be miles away, but we know of them already.

[103]

May the fortune of the reign of His Grand Majesty

Be improved by God—this be our only entreaty.

By God, this has been an excellent festive assembly!

O 'Jan'! What powers do you have to write its eulogy?

A million events remain which could not be versified,

Those themes, despite everything, remain unversified.

Editor's Note and Acknowledgements

The *Musaddas tahniyat-e-jashn-e-benazir* manuscript preserved at the Rampur Raza Library has remained a valuable source of information among the scholarly community. It has been consulted by historians, ethnomusicologists and literary scholars, among others. The Rampur Raza Library has published a facsimile edition including the Urdu original alongside Nagari transliteration with all the paintings. I wanted to introduce the text to scholars working in English and a wider audience. Keeping this in mind, I have provided a detailed introduction to the text that incorporates a selection of Urdu verses from the original to add a sense of poetic form. Besides attempting a literal translation, the translator has tried to capture the rhyme scheme in English to acquaint English-speaking readers with the nuance and brilliance of this text. Such an approach requires dialogue and collaboration among historians and literary scholars of which this edition is an example.

My first and foremost thanks to Shad Naved for a meaningful collaboration and the many discussions on the text and translation. I am grateful to Patrick French for encouraging me to pursue this project. Meru Gokhale and Premanka Goswami have been exemplary and supportive editors at Penguin Random House India. I have learnt from my conversations and comments offered by Sunil Sharma and Carla Petievich on the introduction. To develop this engagement further, I am also collaborating with scriptwriter, Danish Iqbal, and performance artist, Fouzia Dastango, to adapt this text for the revival of Rekhti performance. It has been the most rewarding learning experience so far in working with the Rekhti voice. I want to acknowledge the support of the director, librarian Abu Saad Islahi and staff members Sanam Khan, Syed Tareq Azhar of Rampur Raza Library who have helped by granting permission and providing copies of images, one of which is used on this book's cover. Last, but not the least, this text is a tribute to the life and work of Mir Yar Ali 'Jan Sahib', and I hope that this edition will bring further scholarly and popular attention to his works.

—Razak Khan

Translator's Note and Acknowledgements

Justifying his rejection of rhyme in his epic English poem, John Milton's words 'Rhyme being no necessary adjunct or true ornament of poem or good verse, in longer works especially, [is] but the invention of a barbarous age' have the ring of near absolute truth among poets and translators today. That 'barbarous age', however, does not seem to have ended in literary cultures which practise rhyme as one of the key formal features of verse. The 'eastern' poetic genres, especially the ghazal, masnavi, qasida and marsiya, have living practitioners today who have developed ways to remain in rhyme.

With the rise of the English ghazal, in recent years, the question of rhyme is once again upon us. We seem to tolerate rhyme as a quaint remnant of other, non-English writing, even accept it as a breath of fresh air in the rambling extensiveness of English free verse. But perhaps the severest banishment of rhyme in recent years has occurred in translations from the Arabic, Persian and Urdu languages in which the orthodoxy of rhymed verse has prevailed for centuries. Milton's complaint against 'the jingling sound' of rhyme is taken all too seriously by translators when they render ghazals, masnavis and qasidas in free verse, or worse, summary in prose. While this choice could have aesthetic (perhaps to render the freshness of an old sensibility in more modern form) and/or disciplinary motives (perhaps to render literature more readable for writers of history), it has the profound result of serving a global language of English translation. A new orthodoxy replaces the old one.

In this translation of Jan Sahib's *Jashn-e-Benazir*, one of the last long poems in the Rekhti voice from pre-modern Urdu literary culture, I have chosen to represent the original's rhyme scheme. The reason for this is *not* fidelity to the original. In its particular case, the lengthy poem hangs together on the armature of rhyme and metre. It does not tell a story or elaborate a philosophical theme, like the famous Persian and Urdu masnavis; it is a musaddas (a poem in six-line stanzas) used for commemorative or hortatory verse. As Annemarie Schimmel tells us, the musaddas is itself a late-classical form which reached its fruition during the late nineteenth century. Rhyme played a crucial role in the marching rhythm of Hali's call to the faithful to reform their civilization in musaddas stanzas and Iqbal's famous dialogues, again in musaddas stanzas, with the transcendental. Jan Sahib's poem, by contrast, is light, textured and full of pizzazz. Yet, its aspiration is no less serious than Hali's or Iqbal's, as the choice of the musaddas stanza suggests. During the political decline of Indo–Persianate literary culture, Jan Sahib's commemorative poem seeks to present a word-album that must hold together for its readers not just as nostalgia but as a continuous, living pageant of poetry and the various arts (visual, musical, erotic, culinary, architectural). This album is held together by its basic rhyme scheme: AAAABB, that is, the first four lines rhyme and the last two have a different rhyme in each stanza. I have maintained this scheme in my translation. The rhymes are not always perfect; the reader will find all the major kinds of rhymes (masculine, feminine, slant, near, eye) strewn across the translation. In a few dire cases, such as the opening stanza, a repeated end-word is made to stand in for rhyme (just as Jan Sahib himself switches between rhyme and rhyme-plus-refrain in some stanzas). The point of the rhyme scheme is to define for the reader the spine of this book-length poem. While each stanza shows an internal unity of theme, purpose and conceit, the stanzas are linked to each other by the six-line format, its internal rhyme and uniform metre. A further challenge would be to produce a uniform English metrical line in translation. The present translation stops at an echo of the Urdu metrical line and rhythm to be heard faintly in only some of the lines.

In preparing this translation, I benefitted from the collation of textual variants by Mohammad Mubeen Asif, who worked as research assistant with me on the 'Poetry in the Indo–Islamic Millennium: From Manuscript to Teaching Tools' project (2017–19) funded generously by Ambedkar University Delhi. Discussions on the project with my co-principal investigators, Mrityunjay Tripathi and Awadhesh Kumar Tripathi, have shaped my idea of translation practised here. I thank Razak Khan for giving me free rein as translator and not insisting on mimetic prosiness for his edition of the poem. Any errors of reading, interpretation and translation remain mine alone.

—Shad Naved

Bibliography

Ahmed, Shahab, *What Is Islam? The Importance of Being Islamic*, Princeton, NJ: Princeton University Press, 2016.

Bayly, C.A., *Rulers Townsmen and Bazaars: North Indian Society in the Age of British Expansion 1770–1870*, Cambridge: Cambridge University Press, 1983.

Behl, Aditya, 'Poet of the Bazaars: Nazir Akbarabadi, 1735–1830', in Kathryn Hansen and David Lelyveld (eds), *A Wilderness of Possibilities: Urdu Studies in Transnational Perspective*, Delhi: Oxford University Press, 2005.

Iqbal, Muhammad, *Taking Issue & Allah's Answer: Shikwa and Jawaab-e-Shikwa*, Mustansir Dalvi (trans.), New Delhi: Penguin Books, 2012.

Jan Sahib, Mir Yar Ali, *Musaddas tahniyat-e-jashn-e-benazir*, W.H. Siddiqi and Imtiaz Ali Khandara (eds), Rampur: Raza Library Publications, 1999.

Jan Sahib, Mir Yar Ali, *Musaddas tahniyat-e-jashn-e-benazir*, Muhammad Ali Khan Asar Rampuri (ed.), Rampur: State Press, 1950.

Jan Sahib, Mir Yar Ali, *Dīvan-e-Jan Jan Ṣaḥib: ma' farhang-e-mufīdah*, Niẓami Badayuni (ed.), Badayun: Niẓami Press, 1923.

Naim, C.M., 'Transvestic Words? The *Rekhti* in Urdu', *Annual of Urdu Studies,* 16 (2001), pp. 3–26.

Platts, John Thompson, *A Dictionary of Urdu, Classical Hindi, and English*, London: W.H. Allen & Co., 1884.

Petievich, Carla, '*Rekhti:* Impersonating the Feminine in Urdu Poetry', *South Asia: Journal of South Asian Studies*, 24 (2001), pp. 75–90.

Sangari, Kumkum, 'Multiple Temporalities, Unsettled Boundaries, Trickster Women: Reading a Nineteenth-Century *Qissa*', in Vasudha Dalmia and Stuart Blackburn (eds), *India's Literary History: Essays on the Nineteenth Century*, Delhi: Permanent Black, 2003.

Schimmel, Annemarie, *Classical Urdu Literature from the Beginning to Iqbal*, Wiesbaden: O. Harrassowitz, 1975.

Sen, Sudipta, 'Passages of Authority: Rulers, Traders and Marketplaces in Bengal and Benares, 1700–1750', *The Calcutta Historical Journal*, 17: 1 (1996), pp. 1–39.

Shackle, Christopher and Javed Majeed, *Hali's Musaddas: The Flow and Ebb of Islam*, Delhi: Oxford University Press, 1997.

Sharma, Sunil, 'If There Is a Paradise on Earth, It Is Here: Urban Ethnography in Indo-Persian Poetic and Historical Texts', in Sheldon Pollock (ed.), *Forms of Knowledge in Early Modern Asia*, Durham: Duke University Press, 2011.

Vanita, Ruth, *Gender, Sex and the City: Urdu Rekhti Poetry in India 1700–1870*, New York: Palgrave Macmillan, 2012.

Yang, Anand, *The Limited Raj: Agrarian Relations in Colonial India*, Berkeley: University of California Press, 1989.

Notes

1   Ruth Vanita, *Gender, Sex and the City: Urdu Rekhti Poetry in India 1700–1870*, New York: Palgrave Macmillan, 2012, p. 258.

2   Platts, John T. A *Dictionary of Urdu, Classical Hindi, and English*, London: W.H. Allen & Co., 1884, p. 611.

3   Vanita, *Gender, Sex and the City*, p. 213.

4   Carla Petievich, '*Rekhti:* Impersonating the feminine in Urdu poetry', *South Asia: Journal of South Asian Studies*, 24 (2001), pp. 75-90; C.M. Naim, 'Transvestic Words? The Rekhti in Urdu', *Annual of Urdu Studies,* 16 (2001), Part 1, pp. 3–26.

5   Mir Yar Ali Jan Sahib, *Musaddas tahniyat-e-jashn-e-be-nazir*, W.H. Siddiqi and Imtiaz Ali Khan Khandara (eds), Rampur: Raza Library Publications, 1999.

6   Jan Sahib, *Musaddas*, p. 7.

7   Aditya Behl, 'Poet of the Bazaars: Nazir Akbarabadi, 1735–1830', in Kathryn Hansen and David Lelyveld (eds), *A Wilderness of Possibilities: Urdu Studies in Transnational Perspective*, Delhi: Oxford University Press, 2005, p. 205.

8   Sudipta Sen, 'Passages of Authority: Rulers, Traders and Marketplaces in Bengal and Benares, 1700–1750', *The Calcutta Historical Journal*, 17: 1, 1996, p. 19.

9   C.A. Bayly, *Rulers, Townsmen and Bazaars: North Indian Society in the Age of British Expansion 1770–1870*, Cambridge: Cambridge University Press, 1983.

10 Anand Yang, *The Limited Raj: Agrarian Relations in Colonial India*, Berkeley: University of California Press, 1989, p. 152.

11 Sunil Sharma has traced the genealogy of the 'lyrical verse with ethnographic overtones' in Indo–Persian texts. See, Sunil Sharma, 'If There Is a Paradise on Earth, It Is Here: Urban Ethnography in Indo–Persian Poetic and Historical Texts', in Sheldon Pollock (ed.), *Forms of Knowledge in Early Modern Asia*, Durham: Duke University Press, 2011, p. 241.

12 Jan Sahib, *Musaddas*, p. 31.

13 Ibid., p. 80.

14 Kumkum Sangari, 'Multiple Temporalities, Unsettled Boundaries, Trickster Women: Reading a Nineteenth-century *Qissa*', in Vasudha Dalmia and Stuart

Blackburn (eds), I*ndia's Literary History: Essays on the Nineteenth Century*, Delhi: Permanent Black, 2003, pp. 239–40.

15 These translations are based on the canonical colonial Urdu dictionary by Platts that continues to remain influential among Urdu scholars. John Thompson Platts, *A Dictionary of Urdu, Classical Hindi, and English*, 1884, p. 1123. (Available online at the University of Chicago's Digital South Asia Library website:
http://dsal.uchicago.edu/dictionaries/platts/frontmatter/frontmatter.html).

16. Mir Yar Ali Jan Sahib, *Divan-e-Jan Sahib: ma' farhang-e-mufidah*, Nizami Badayuni (ed.), Badayun: Nizami Press, 1923.

17 Jan Sahib, *Musaddas*, p. 115.

18 Ibid., p. 113.

19 Ibid., p. 115.

20 Ibid., p. 117.

21 Ibid., p. 123.

22 Ibid., p. 125.

23 Ibid., p. 157.

24 Ibid., pp. 123–27.

25. Mir Yar Ali Jan Sahib, *Musaddas tahniyat-e-jashn-e-benazir*, Muhammad Ali Khan Asar Rampuri (ed.), Rampur: State Press, 1950.

26 Ibid., pp. 117–20.

27 Jan Sahib, *Musaddas*, Ibid., p. 120.

28 Ibid., p. 131.

29 Ibid., p. 73.

30 Ibid., p. 127.

31 Ibid., p. 39.

32. Mir Yar Ali Jan Sahib, *Musaddas tahniyat-e-jashn-e-benazir*, Muhammad Ali Khan Asar Rampuri (ed.), Rampur: State Press, 1950.

33 Jan, *Mussadas*, p. 79.

34 Ibid., p. 101.

35 Ibid., p. 129.

36 Ibid., p. 131.

37 Ibid., p. 133.

38 Ibid., p. 141.

39 Ibid., p. 143.

40 Ibid., p. 145.

41 Ibid., p. 159.

42 Ibid., p. 161.

43 Ibid., p. 59.

44 Ibid., p. 100.

45 Ibid.

46 Ibid., p. 88.

47 Shahab Ahmed, *What Is Islam? The Importance of Being Islamic*, Princeton, NJ: Princeton University Press, 2016, p. 32. For Ahmed, it is both a temporal-

geographical entity ranging from the fifteenth to the late nineteenth century. In the 'vast geographical region extending from the Balkans through Anatolia, Iran and Central Asia down and across Afghanistan and North India to the Bay of Bengal that was home to the absolute demographic majority of Muslims of planet'.